THIS BOOK BELONGS TO:

MY AWESOME PRESHCOOL WORKBOOK

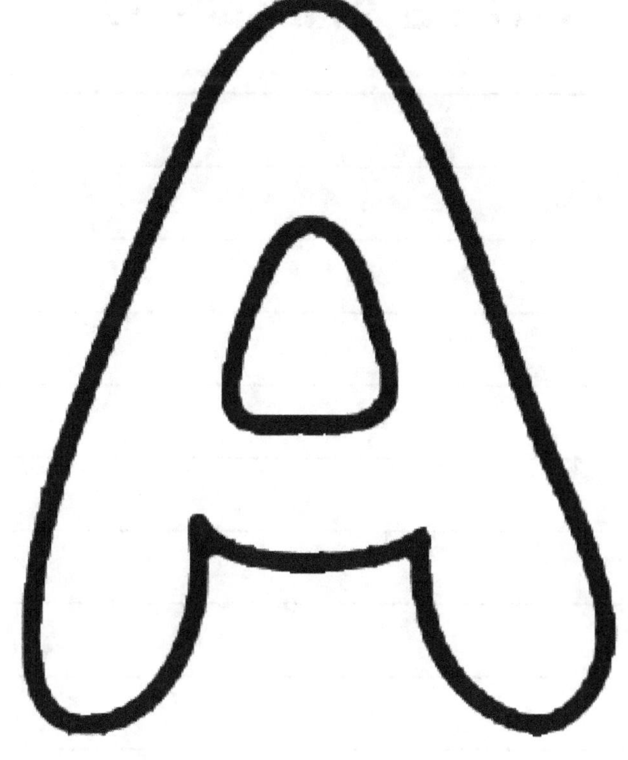

A APPLE

WRITE AND DRAW

B

BOOK

WRITE AND DRAW

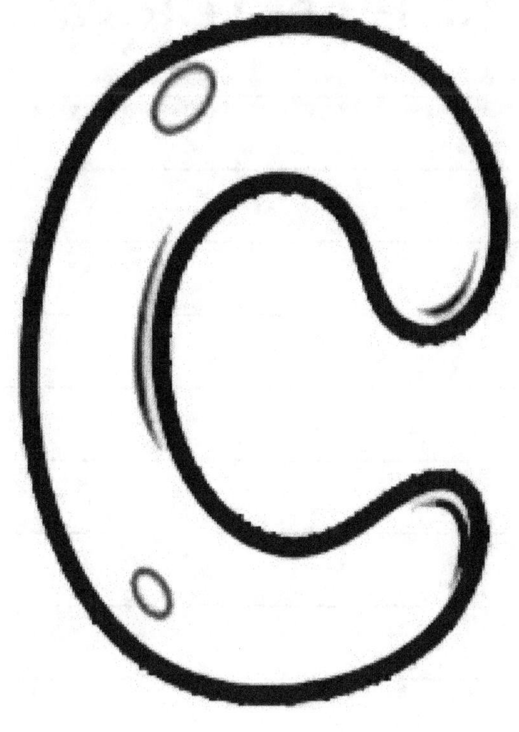

C   CLOWN

WRITE AND DRAW

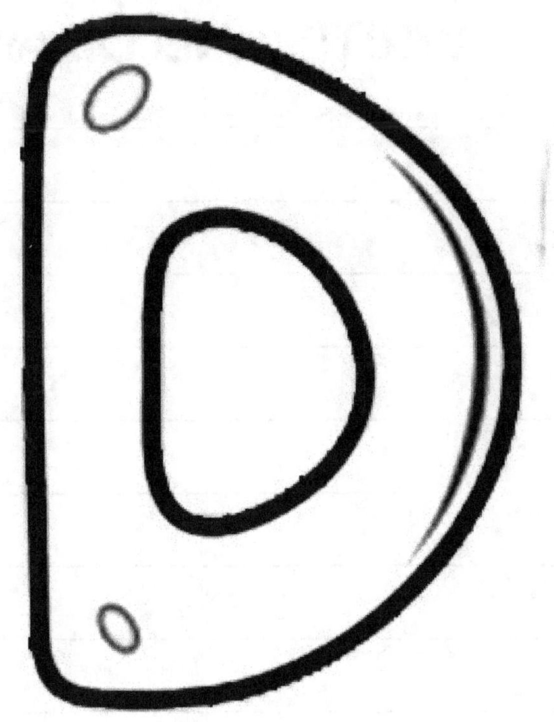

D

DOLPHIN

WRITE AND DRAW

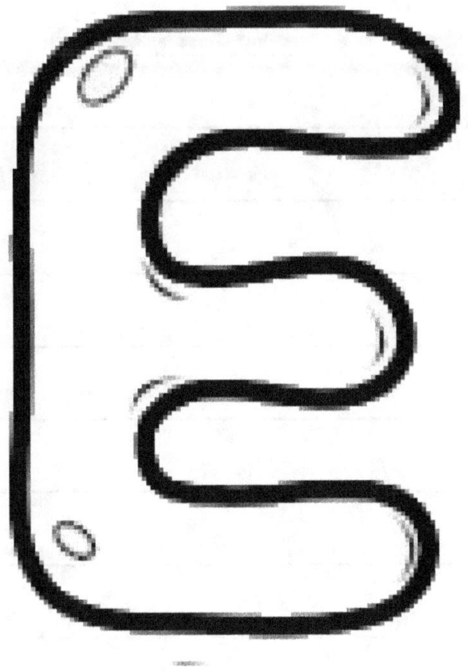

E   ELEPHANT

WRITE AND DRAW

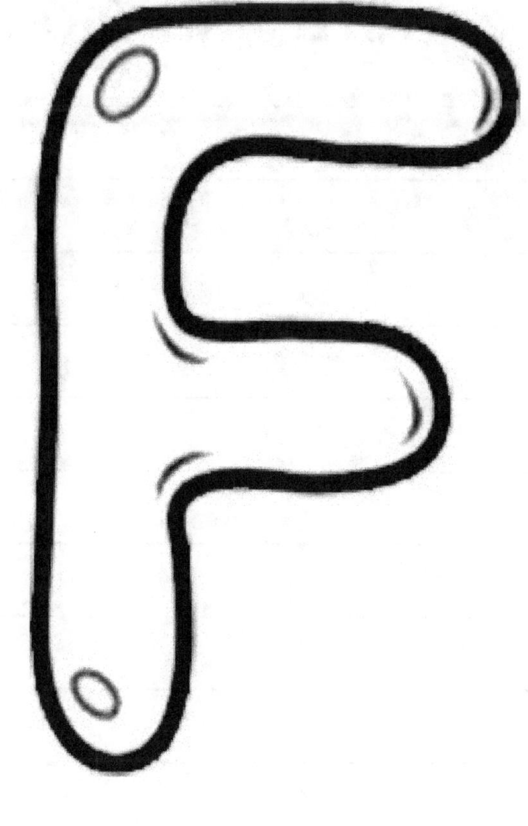

F

FISH

WRITE AND DRAW

G

GORILLA

WRITE AND DRAW

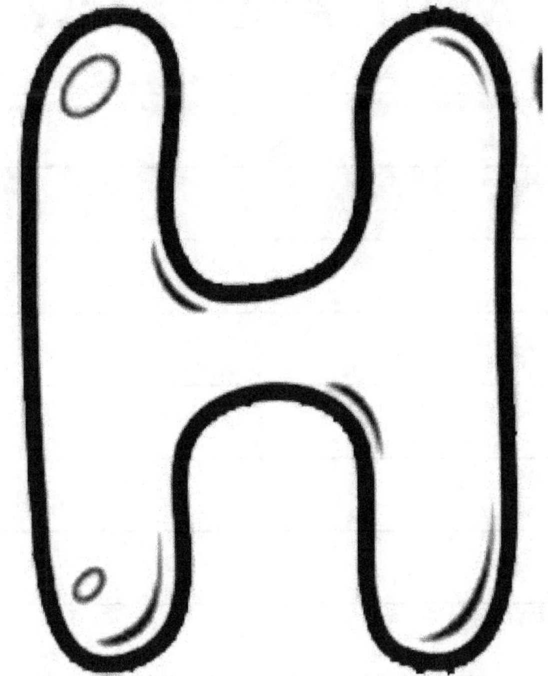

H

HAT

WRITE AND DRAW

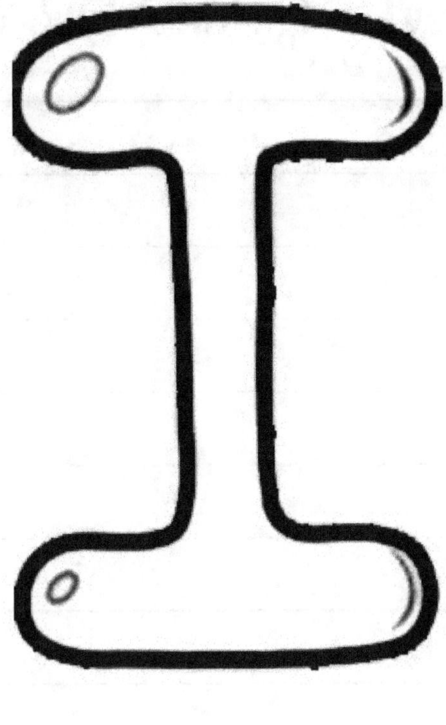

I

ICE

WRITE AND DRAW

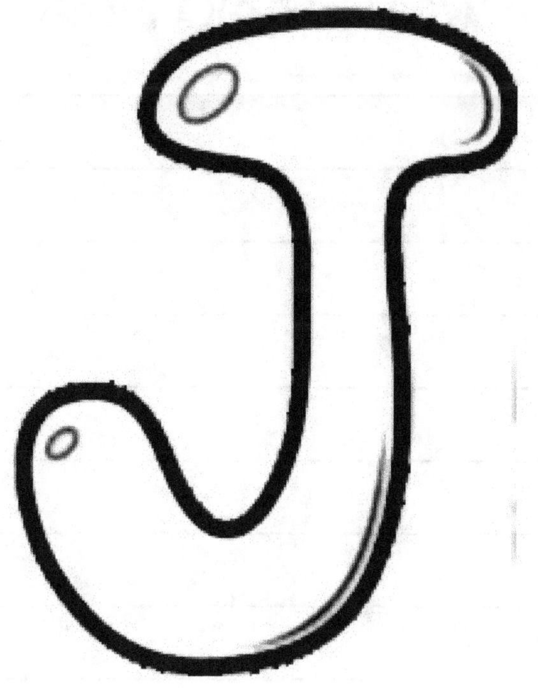

J

JACKET

WRITE AND DRAW

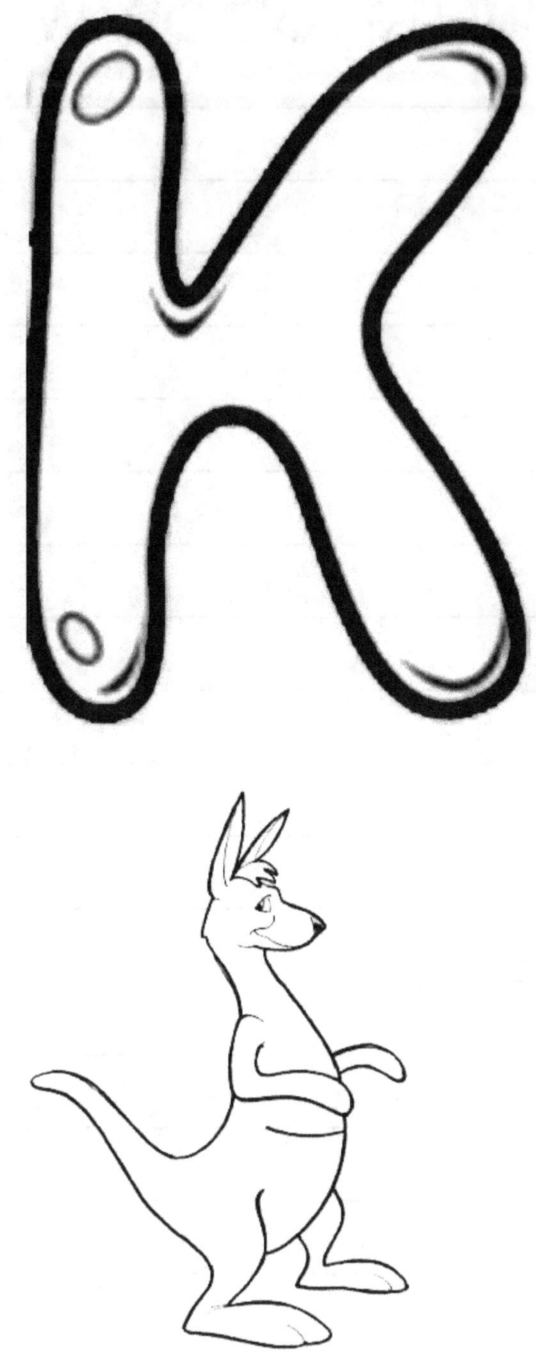

K   KANGORO

WRITE AND DRAW

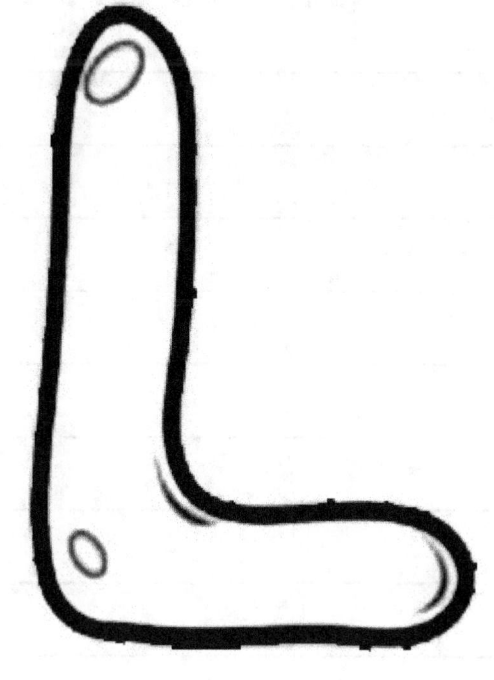

L LION

WRITE AND DRAW

M

MONKEY

WRITE AND DRAW

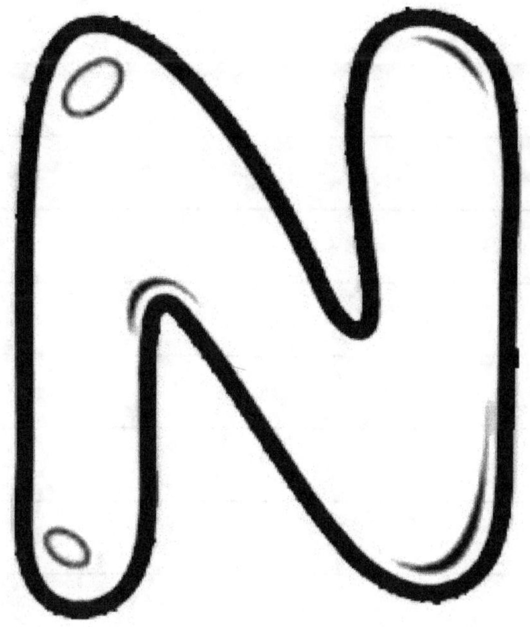

N

NOTEBOOK

WRITE AND DRAW

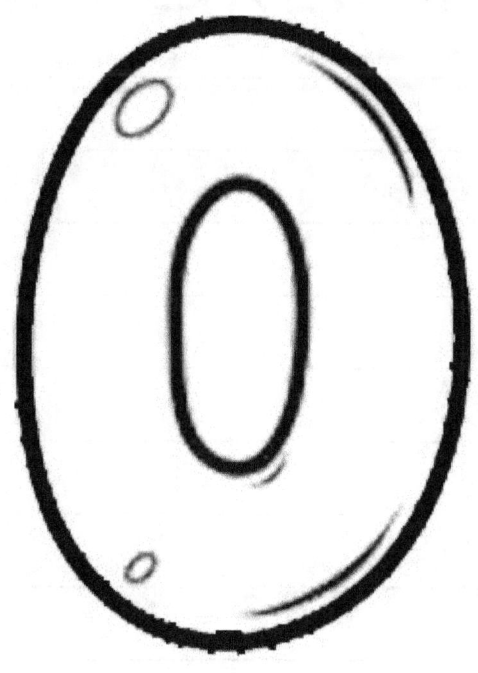

O

OWL

WRITE AND DRAW

P

PEAR

WRITE AND DRAW

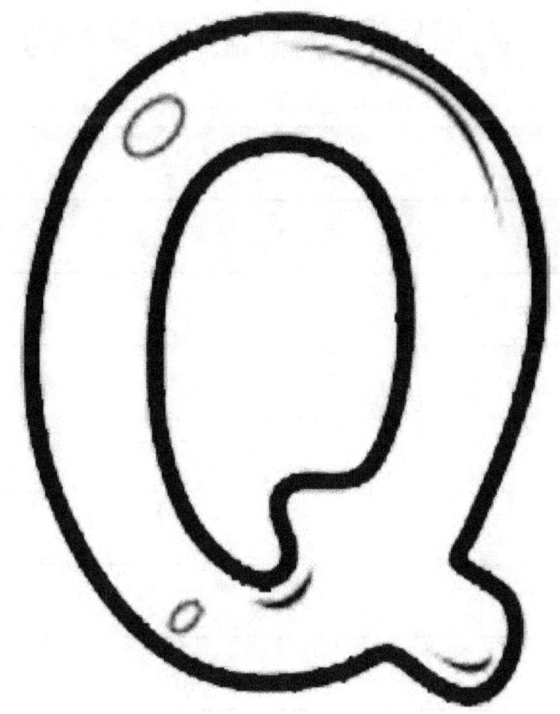

Q

QUEEN

WRITE AND DRAW

R

WRITE AND DRAW

S

WRITE AND DRAW

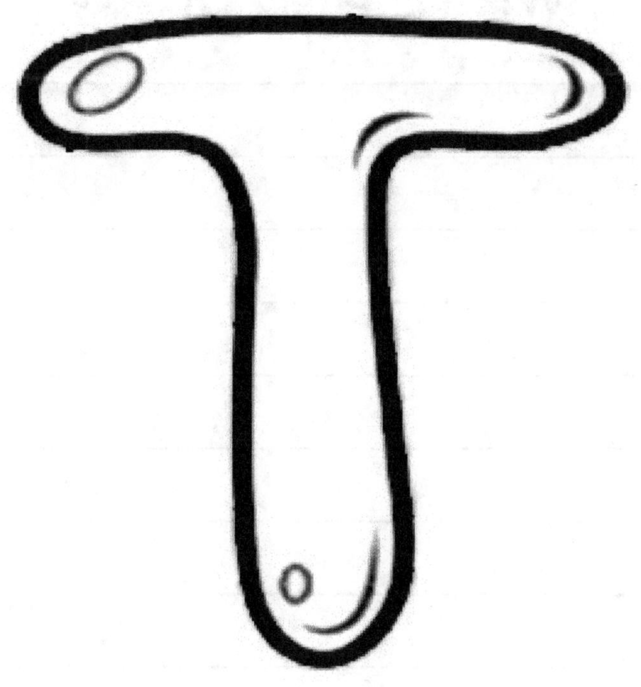

T

TORTOISE

WRITE AND DRAW

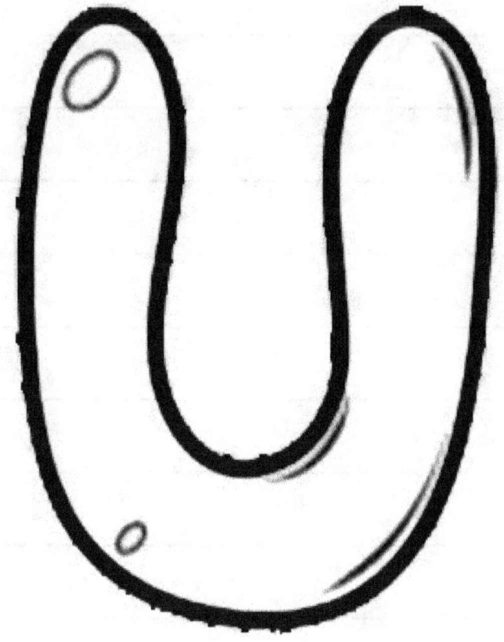

U

UMBRELLA

WRITE AND DRAW

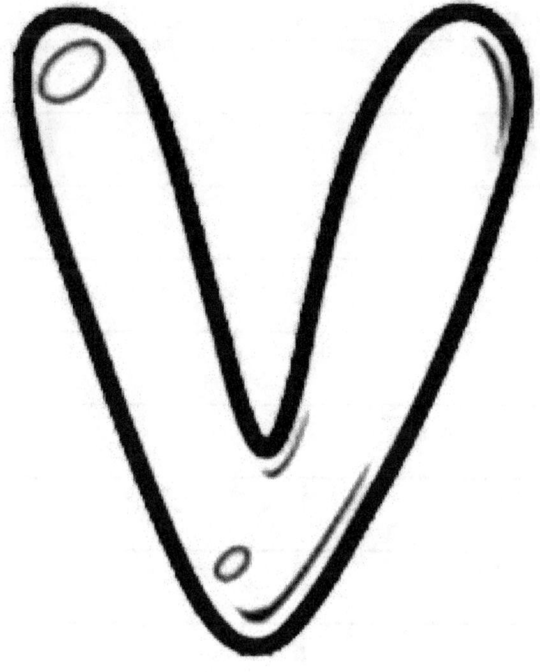

V

V A N

WRITE AND DRAW

W

WEB

WRITE AND DRAW

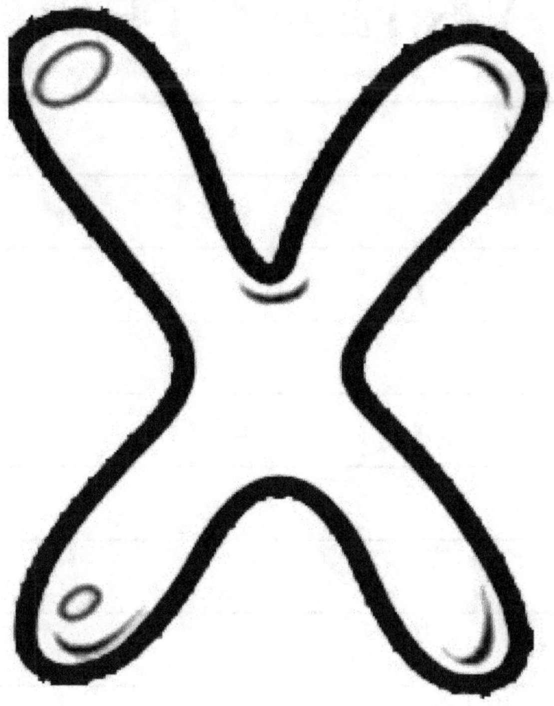

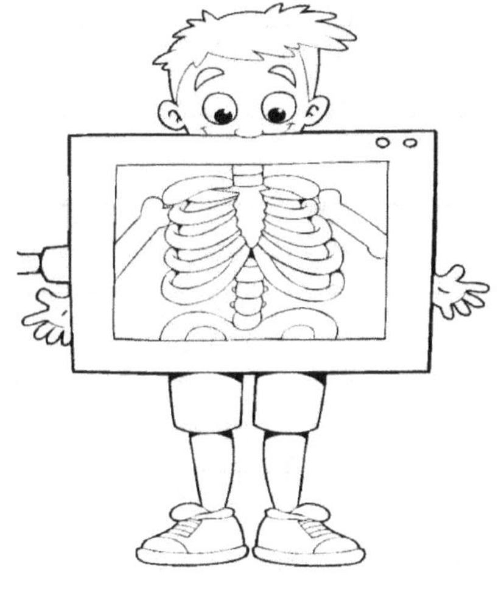

X

WRITE AND DRAW

z ZEBRA

WRITE AND DRAW

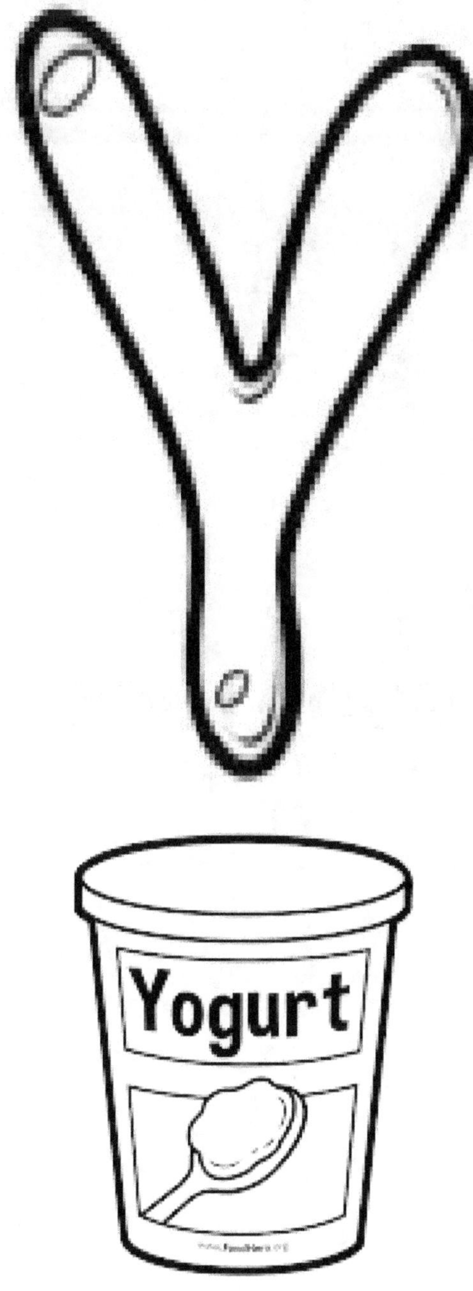

Y YAGURT

GOOD LUCK